The Outdoor Adventure Handbook

The Outdoor Adventure Handbook

Hugh McManners

DK

DORLING KINDERSLEY
London • New York • Stuttgart

A DORLING KINDERSLEY BOOK

Editor Patricia Grogan **Art Editor** Lesley Betts

Project Editor Fiona Robertson

Photography Andy Crawford

Production Charlotte Traill

Deputy Editorial Director Sophie Mitchell
Deputy Art Director Miranda Kennedy

The outdoor adventurers:
Nadia Barak, Jessie Clark, Ryan Davies,
Johnathan Green, Sayed Meah, Lauren Shaw

First published in Great Britain in 1996 by
Dorling Kindersley Limited,
9 Henrietta Street, London WC2E 8PS
Reprinted 1996 (twice)

A CIP catalogue record for this book is available from the British Library

ISBN 0 7513 5382 5

Colour reproduction by Colourscan, Singapore
Printed in Hong Kong by Wing King Tong

The author would like to dedicate this book to his two
sons William and Joseph, with all his love

Contents

How to use this book

This book contains all the information that you need for adventures outdoors. It will help you to understand and avoid the problems that could arise, and ensure that your trips are always safe and successful. Enjoy your adventures!

Getting out

Planning is the key to a successful trip. Think carefully about what you are going to do and what you will need. The more trips you go on, the more experienced you will become, but for now, this book gives you the best possible start!

Look on page 8 to find out how to roll your clothes, ready for packing them in your backpack.

Page 13 will show you how to carry your backpack safely.

Find out what to avoid at your campsite on page 14.

Learn how to organize everything inside your tent on page 18.

Setting up camp

When choosing a campsite, you need to know how to look for a safe, comfortable site, and how to recognize the kinds of places to avoid. Trying to move a wrongly placed camp at night is very inconvenient, and could even be dangerous.

Cooking outdoors

For delicious meals and enjoyable evenings, it is hard to beat a campfire. However, fires can spread easily, so it is important that you learn how to build and light them safely. When handling hot liquids and food you should also ensure that you use the right equipment to avoid burning yourself.

Build a wigwam fire following the instructions on page 24.

Try some of the alternative cooking methods shown on page 27.

Look on page 33 for how to make a stool for your camp.

Page 34 shows you how to ensure that you always have clean water in your camp.

Living outdoors

If you are going to live outdoors for a while, you could make equipment for your camp. It is also important to camp near a supply of water because you will not be able to take all the water you need with you.

Navigation outdoors

Being able to find your way, or navigate, accurately is an important outdoor skill. It stops you getting lost and also enables you to reach your destination by other routes. Once you have learned how to read a map correctly, you can even try making your own!

Make your own compass by following the instructions on page 37.

Learn what a route card is used for and how to make one on page 40.

Learn the difference between a hopping print and a wading print on page 48.

Predict the weather using the clouds on page 50.

Observing nature

Nature can provide you with many clues about your environment. For example, plants can show which direction to take and insects can indicate where the nearest water is. Even the clouds in the sky can help you to predict the weather.

Important techniques

Using a knife, tying knots, and basic first aid are techniques that you have to learn how to do properly. This book contains detailed sections showing you exactly what you need to know – particularly how to look after someone who is injured.

Learn how to sharpen a penknife on page 53.

Find out when and how to put someone in the recovery position on page 61.

Find groups in your area that organize outdoor activities on page 63.

The index on page 64 shows you where to find everything in this book.

Reference pages

The outdoors is a wonderful place, which must be looked after very carefully so that we can enjoy it, and also so that others may have as much fun as we do. The Countryside Code tells you exactly how to do this.

How to use each page

Each double-page in this book tells you everything you need to know about one subject. The introduction gives you an overview, and the step-by-step instructions show you how to make and do everything.

Star symbol
This symbol appears next to important safety points.

Knot symbol
You will see this symbol when you need to tie a knot.

Penknife symbol
Every time you need to use a penknife, you will see this symbol.

Locator picture
This picture sums up what is being shown on the page.

Materials box
Look here to find the materials you need.

Ecology points
These symbols are found next to points about your environment.

Hints and tips
Each hints and tips box is packed with useful informaton.

Boot-print symbol
This symbol appears next to useful tips.

Step-by-step instructions show you how to make items for your outdoor adventures.

Hints and tips boxes have a picture of a boy or girl.

Boxed instructions
These instructions give you details on how to make and do the activities.

Extra information
At the bottom of most right-hand pages, you will find additional or new information about the subject.

Water- and wind-proof jackets keep you dry and protected from the wind.

Outdoor clothes

The secret of being warm in the cold and cool in the heat is to wear lots of thin layers of loose-fitting clothes. Air is trapped between each layer of clothes and is warmed up by your body heat. You can add or remove layers if you start to feel cold or warm. Trapping your body heat in this way is called insulation.

Packing your winter kit

Pack several layers of underwear, T-shirts, and shirts. Lots of thin, loose clothes are better than a few thick, bulky ones that are difficult to dry out.

Warm, loose-fitting trousers are vital.

Take plenty of vests.

Pack two or three long-sleeved shirts.

Long johns are good for sleeping in.

A warm woollen jumper is ideal for wearing in cool evenings.

Pack several pairs of pants.

Take several pairs of thick woollen or cotton socks.

Wear walking boots or sturdy shoes.

A spare pair of lighter shoes is very useful.

How to roll your clothes for packing them in your backpack

Lay your clothes out flat in an oblong shape. If you are folding a top, fold the sleeves inwards.

Starting at the bottom, roll up each item of clothing. Do not roll the clothes too tightly.

Your rolled clothes will take up less room in your backpack, and should not get too creased.

Hints and tips

Avoid wearing long johns when you are walking because they may make you too hot.

When you are resting, do not forget to put on extra layers and a warm hat before you start feeling cold.

Wet weather clothes

You need clothes that will keep you dry but will not make you sweat.

Lace secures gaiter to your leg.

Gaiters stop water running into your boots and making your feet wet.

Wear waterproof trousers around your camp, especially when you are kneeling on the ground.

Wear gaiters when walking in wet weather. Unlike waterproof trousers, they will not make you sweat.

Winter clothes

Wear lots of thin layers. The outer layers should have zips so that you can open them if you get too hot.

A peaked hat keeps the sun off your face.

A warm hat is vital – up to half your body heat is lost through your head and shoulders.

Gloves and a scarf will keep you warm.

Watch out for water running off your jacket and on to your trousers and socks.

Wear two pairs of socks when it is very cold.

Summer clothes

Shorts and T-shirts are great for warm weather, but in hot sunshine wear light, long-sleeved tops and trousers.

Wear plenty of sun block in sunny weather.

Loose-fitting cotton T-shirt

Wear light colours in very hot weather to reflect the heat.

Thick socks will make your boots more comfortable.

How to protect your neck from the Sun using a tea towel

Place the tea towel over your head, making sure it covers the sides and back of your neck.

Put a peaked cap on over the tea towel. The brim of the cap will protect your face.

Secure the tea towel by carefully pinning safety pins around the bottom of the cap.

If it is very hot, soak the tea towel in cold water first.

Packing your summer kit

You need fewer layers in the summer than in the winter, and light, cotton clothes are ideal. But remember to pack warm clothes too, for when it gets cold at night.

Pack long- and short-sleeved tops.

Take a few cotton vests.

Take a warm jumper for the evenings.

Pack several pairs of cotton pants.

Lightweight trousers will dry out easily if they get wet.

Spare shoes; trainers are ideal.

Shorts are ideal for warm days.

Wear walking boots or sturdy shoes.

Thick, woollen socks will insulate your feet from hot ground.

Your outdoor kit

It is easy to pack too much, and it is very hard to carry it all. Think carefully about what you are going to do, then take only the bare minimum. Your survival kit is your most important kit, so always allow room for it in your backpack. Try to find several different uses for everything else that you take with you.

If in doubt, you probably do not need it, so leave it out.

Your survival kit

This is the most important kit to take with you. Keep it in waterproof containers and make sure you know where everything is at all times.

Take a whistle to attract someone's attention.

Compass

Notebook

Waterproof pen

Torch

Penknife

Pack a magnifying glass for studying wildlife.

Pack a needle and thread to make repairs.

Take string and rope for making equipment.

Candle

Torch batteries

Matches

Remember to take some emergency money with you.

Your shelter kit

This kit will keep you warm and dry, so it is important to look after it carefully.

A first aid kit is vital on all trips.

Use bin-liners to make your backpack waterproof.

Keep the tent poles together.

Sleeping bag

Check the tent has no holes in it before setting off.

A sleeping mat will keep you warm at night.

A sheet to make a sheet bag.

Take a ground sheet if your tent does not have one.

Your cooking kit

A wooden spoon, mug, plate, cooking pot with a lid, and a tin opener are all you really need to take. However, if you have got room, take foil with you to wrap and cook food in.

Take a billy can set – cooking pots with a lid and handle.

Foil is always handy.

Fork

Pack a pan holder if your billy can set does not have a handle.

A wooden spatula is useful for lifting fish off a grill.

A water bottle is always useful.

Spoon   *Knife*   *Wooden spoon*

Tin opener

Use a bowl for soup and cereal.

Plastic plates do not heat up as quickly as metal plates.

Take a plastic mug for hot drinks.

Bowl   *Plate*

Washing up kit

Wash up after every meal. It is important to keep everything clean, so you do not attract animals.

Washing up liquid

Scouring pad   *Tea towel to dry up with*

A bowl to wash up in

Your wash kit

Do not forget to pack your wash kit. Keep it all together in a clean waterproof bag.

Packing items such as your shampoo in small containers will save space in your backpack.

Wash bag   *Towel*

Hair brush

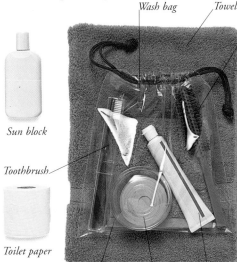

Sun block

Shampoo

Toothbrush

Toilet paper

Talcum powder to help prevent foot blisters.

Flannel   *Toothpaste*

Soap

Packing your outdoor kit

Make sure everything in your backpack is waterproof by packing it in plastic bags. Group things you use together in the same bag so that you can find them easily. Pack all of these bags inside your lined backpack; if they are attached to the outside, they could fall off or get damaged.

Line your backpack with two large bin-liners to make it waterproof.

How to pack your kit

The main rules to remember are to put the heaviest things at the top of your backpack, the lightest, bulkiest things at the bottom, and the things that you need to get at quickly in the side pockets. Pack your sleeping bag in the bottom of your backpack first. Remember to wrap it in a waterproof bag. Place other light items, such as your clothes, on top and then add the heavy items, such as the tent poles.

Weekend packs
Use a smaller pack for shorter trips, as you will not need to take so much with you.

Backpacks
Choose a backpack that is not too large, otherwise you may be tempted to pack too much and will not be able to carry it all.

Cooking equipment, such as a billy can set, is a heavy item.

Toilet paper

Keep the first aid kit handy at all times.

Keep your wash kit together in a waterproof bag.

Plates

Water bottle

Sun block

Pack your survival kit in the side pockets, so you can get to it easily.

Penknife

Whistle

Keep your backpack full, so the heavy items stay at the top.

Pack the heavy tent poles higher than your clothes, which are lighter.

Tent poles and pegs should be packed in the same bag.

Pack things inside each other to save space.

Pack string and rope for making equipment.

Use soft items to pad out the back of your backpack.

Pack spare shoes with the soles facing outwards.

Roll your clothes and pack them in plastic bags.

⭐ Make sure there are no sharp edges digging into your back.

The bottom of the backpack is filled out with the sleeping bag.

How to make a kit bag to carry lighter items

Wrap some string around a pebble placed in the corner of a strong bag and tie two half-hitch knots.

Join the string to 1 m (3 ft) of thick rope by tying them together with a sheet bend knot.

Pack everything evenly into the bag. Gather the top of the bag and place a pebble on top.

Fold over the top of the bag, wrap some string around the pebble, and tie two half-hitch knots.

Tie this string to the rope with a sheet bend knot. Sling the bag diagonally across your back.

See page 55 for tying a half-hitch knot and a sheet bend knot.

Making a kit bag

You never know when you may need an extra bag. Follow the instructions on the left to make a kit bag that you can use on short day trips, or for collecting fire wood.

Make sure everything is spread out evenly through the bag.

Avoid sharp items that may make a hole in the bag.

You can buy special backpack liners, which are ideal for making kit bags.

Pad the shoulder strap of the kit bag with leaves.

Carrying your backpack

Backpacks are often heavy. Because of this, it is important to carry them correctly so that you do not hurt yourself. Adjust your pack so that it is as high up as possible to stop the weight pulling on your shoulders.

Adjustable straps allow the backpack to be carried high on the back.

Tighten and loosen the shoulder straps whenever you feel uncomfortable.

Waist belts help keep the weight off your shoulders.

When walking downhill or crossing rivers, undo the waist belt in case you stumble and have to drop the backpack.

How to make matches waterproof with wax candles

Using a lighted candle, drip wax over the heads of a box of matches, laid side-by-side.

When the wax has cooled, separate each match. Before using them, scrape the wax off the head of each match.

You may need to ask an adult to help you.

How to adjust a backpack to make it comfortable

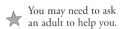

To open the waist belt, squeeze in the side of the buckle with the "teeth". This will release the clasp.

To tighten your waist belt, hold the buckle and pull the strap to the side until the belt is secure.

Tighten the shoulder straps by lifting the edge of the buckle up and pulling the strap down.

Choosing your campsite

It is very important to choose a safe and comfortable place for your campsite, even if you are only going to spend one night outdoors. Look for a dry area, which is slightly raised so that if it rains, the ground will not get boggy. Try also to avoid stony ground, as it is very uncomfortable to sleep on.

Always take the time to find a good spot for your campsite.

If you are camping in the wild, always get permission from the land owner first.

Avoid camping in a basin where cold air or flood water could flow.

Your campsite should be close to a supply of fresh, clean water.

Bushes and low trees will give you shelter from the wind and rain.

Keep food well away from animals and your tent.

Keep food cool by placing it under the shade of a tree.

Choose a windy spot for tying a washing line.

Pack away your clothes as soon as they have finished drying.

If you have a camp toilet, make sure it is downwind from your tent.

Avoid camping in fields with animals.

Flatten the spot you will put up your tent on by removing stones and twigs, and stamping down any lumps.

If you are camping near mountains, do not put up your tent in the path of a possible avalanche or rock-fall.

If you are camping near the sea, avoid low-lying ground where the tide might reach you.

Choosing a tent for the right conditions

Do not put up your tent under trees with branches that could snap off in high winds.

Sleeping on a slope is not easy or comfortable, so try to put up your tent on fairly level ground.

A domed tent is light and spacious. If it is tied down securely, it is ideal for mountainous areas.

Ridge tents, like the one pictured below, are ideal for most conditions.

A tunnel tent can be used on grass or in rocky river valleys. It can withstand high winds.

Ridge tent

Always position your campfire downwind from your tent.

Make sure sparks from your fire cannot reach your tent.

Choose level ground for your cooking area and tent.

Put up your tent so that the entrance faces away from the wind.

Sharing a two-person shelter is not just fun, it will also keep you warm.

Building a shelter

When you are camping outdoors, you may need a shelter to protect you from heavy rain, strong winds, or hot sunshine. If you do not have a tent, you can make this shelter using everyday materials. Put it up on flat ground, in a sheltered place that is protected from the wind.

Materials

Tennis ball cut in half.   *Penknife*

Matches

Sticks   *Ground sheet*

Sheet of plastic

Cord

Pebbles

Stones or bricks

Hints and tips

Always use a torch to light your shelter. Matches and candles can be dangerous – their flames could set fire to your shelter.

In high winds, go outside often to check the cords around the edge of your shelter are tight.

Making your shelter

This two-person shelter can stand on hard or soft ground. It should be wide enough for two people to lie in with their kit.

1 Get a strong sheet of plastic, 2 m x 4 m (6.5 ft x 13 ft). Open it out and lay it on the ground.

See page 54 for tying a reef knot.

2 Attach a cord to each corner and the centre of the longer sides. Use round pebbles to secure the cords, as shown right.

Tie a reef knot in the cords.

You could also attach the cords to tent pegs.   *Leave some cord between the stone and sheet.*

3 Wrap the cords loosely around large stones or bricks to hold the sheet down. Tie half-hitch knots in the wrapped cords to secure them on to the stones or bricks.

How to prepare cords and attach them to your shelter

If you are using cord made of artificial fibres, carefully trim the ends with a penknife.

Melt the ends of the cord with a match. This will seal the fibres together and stop them fraying.

Wrap the sheet around two or three pebbles in the middle of each long side and each corner.

Wrap a piece of cord around the sheet and each set of pebbles. Secure the cord with a reef knot.

How to anchor your shelter and protect the top of it

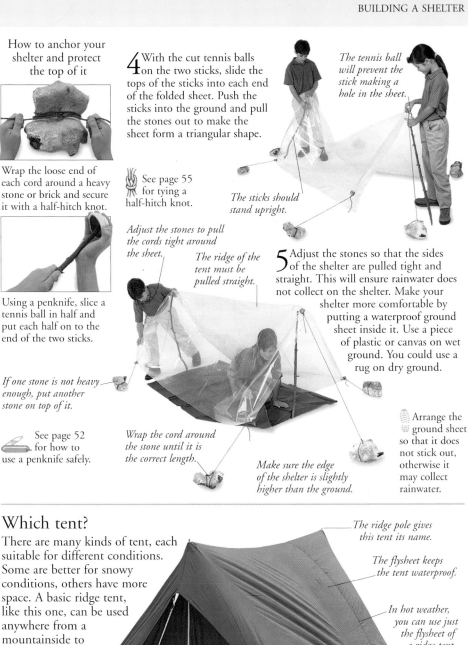

Wrap the loose end of each cord around a heavy stone or brick and secure it with a half-hitch knot.

Using a penknife, slice a tennis ball in half and put each half on to the end of the two sticks.

If one stone is not heavy enough, put another stone on top of it.

See page 52 for how to use a penknife safely.

4 With the cut tennis balls on the two sticks, slide the tops of the sticks into each end of the folded sheet. Push the sticks into the ground and pull the stones out to make the sheet form a triangular shape.

The tennis ball will prevent the stick making a hole in the sheet.

See page 55 for tying a half-hitch knot.

The sticks should stand upright.

Adjust the stones to pull the cords tight around the sheet.

The ridge of the tent must be pulled straight.

5 Adjust the stones so that the sides of the shelter are pulled tight and straight. This will ensure rainwater does not collect on the shelter. Make your shelter more comfortable by putting a waterproof ground sheet inside it. Use a piece of plastic or canvas on wet ground. You could use a rug on dry ground.

Wrap the cord around the stone until it is the correct length.

Make sure the edge of the shelter is slightly higher than the ground.

Arrange the ground sheet so that it does not stick out, otherwise it may collect rainwater.

Which tent?

There are many kinds of tent, each suitable for different conditions. Some are better for snowy conditions, others have more space. A basic ridge tent, like this one, can be used anywhere from a mountainside to your back garden.

The ridge pole gives this tent its name.

The flysheet keeps the tent waterproof.

In hot weather, you can use just the flysheet of a ridge tent.

An elastic loop is useful to tie back the inner tent door.

A small porch is handy for storage space.

A built-in ground sheet will keep water off your sleeping bag.

Look for a full-length zip, which will make it easier to get in and out of the tent.

You need plenty of tent pegs.

Make sure there is strong double-stitching where the guy ropes attach to the flysheet and inner tent.

Living in your camp

To ensure you are comfortable outdoors, you must be well organized and have a place for everything so that nothing gets lost or wet. Whether you are spending just one day or several days outdoors, keep everything that you are not actually using packed, and have set places for everything else.

Hang your boots on sticks pushed into the ground inside your tent porch.

Organizing items in your tent

There is not much room in your tent, so it is important to organize everything carefully. Place things you will need at night close to the head of your sleeping bag and make sure you keep everything else away from the walls of your tent.

Materials

Twigs

Stick

Elastic bands

Penknife

Strong rope for clothes line

Rope for hand rail

Hints and tips

Hanging a torch to the pole at the front of your tent will enable you to light up your tent at night.

When sharing your tent, place the sleeping bags side-by-side with your clothes in the middle.

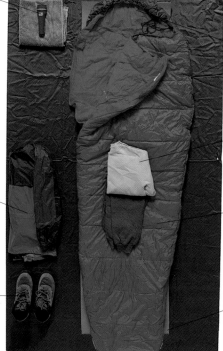

Keep your backpack either in the porch of your tent or just outside.

Have your water bottle handy in case you get thirsty.

Keep any snacks in a sealed bag outside your tent.

Pack away your cooking equipment at night in the porch of your tent.

Put your torch beside your sleeping bag so that you can find it in the dark.

Lay out your sleeping bag with the head facing the door of your tent.

Anything that touches the walls of your tent will get wet, so place your waterproof clothes here.

Place your sleeping clothes inside your sleeping bag.

Store your valuables inside your sleeping bag or under your pillow at night.

Keep your spare shoes at the foot of your tent.

Put your sleeping bag on a foam sleeping mat.

Making a clothes line

It is important to keep everything clean and fresh when you are outdoors, and this includes your clothes. You can use a clothes line not only to dry washed clothes, but also to air everything, including your sleeping bag!

 See page 54 for tying a reef knot.

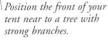

1 Tie one end of the strong rope around your tent pole. Secure the rope with a reef knot.

Use rope that will not stretch when you put clothes on it.

Position the front of your tent near to a tree with strong branches.

Choose a tree far enough away to provide sufficient hanging space for your clothes.

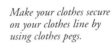

Use your clothes line to air your equipment regularly.

2 Tie the other end of the rope on to a strong branch. Wrap the rope around the branch twice and secure it with a reef knot.

Choose a branch that is about shoulder height.

Your hand rail should be at waist height.

Pull the rope tight.

Hang out your clothes to dry and air on breezy days.

3 With another piece of rope, make a hand rail, which you can use to guide you to the toilet at night. Attach the rope in exactly the same way as you did for the clothes line.

Make your clothes secure on your clothes line by using clothes pegs.

Making a clothes peg

If you do not take clothes pegs with you, or you do not have enough, you can always make some when you are outdoors.

See page 52 for how to use a penknife safely.

1 Find two twigs about 10 cm (2½ in) long. Using a penknife, carefully flatten one long edge of each stick.

2 With the flattened edges facing each other, wrap an elastic band quite tightly around the two sticks.

3 The elastic band will allow you to pull the sticks slightly apart to fit over the clothes line and then spring back again.

Clean and tidy

It is important to keep your camp clean and tidy at all times. An untidy camp quickly becomes uncomfortable and even unhealthy. Animals like ants, squirrels, mice, rats, dogs, and bears will be attracted to any food waste, so always clean and pack everything away as soon as you have finished using it.

Choose a branch that is high enough to lift your larder off the ground.

Materials

Plate

Rope

Plastic bags

Fork

Bin-liners

Pillow case *Tea towel*

Bowl

Hints and tips

Tie the hanging larder on to a branch that is strong enough to hold your food, but will not support an animal's weight.

👣 Store powdery 🐛 foods, such as sugar, salt, pepper, and flour, in airtight containers.

A hanging larder

Keep your food fresh and safe from animals by storing it in a hanging larder.

1 Put the plate into the bottom of the pillow case. This will form the base of the hanging larder.

Check that the food is still sitting on the plate.

2 Wrap the piece of rope around the top of the pillow case twice. This is called two round turns. Now tie the rope together with two half-hitch knots.

See page 55 for tying a half-hitch knot.

Make sure the rope is tied securely to the branch.

Hang in the shade to keep the food cool.

3 Lift the hanging larder off the ground by tying it to a branch or something else that sticks out. Your food will now be safe from animals.

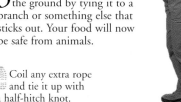

👣 Coil any extra rope 🐛 and tie it up with a half-hitch knot.

More details on how to make the hanging larder

You can use a plate or a bowl. Make sure that it sits flat in the bottom of the pillow case.

Put heavy food, such as potatoes, at the bottom and lighter food, such as peppers, at the top.

When securing the top of the larder, make sure you leave enough rope to tie the larder to a branch.

Tie the larder to a branch with two round turns and two half-hitch knots. Pull the rope tight.

How to make a camp shower using the thick plastic bag

Hang the plastic bag over a branch. Make sure the bag has not got any holes in it.

Fill a bottle with clean water. Now pour the water from the bottle into the plastic bag.

Using a sharp fork or penknife, carefully prick holes along the bottom of the plastic bag.

Quickly jump under the shower before all the water drains out! Fill it up again if you need to.

Keeping drinks cool

You can keep drinks cool by wrapping them in a damp cloth and placing them in a bowl of water in a shady spot. The water in the bowl will keep the cloth wet, which in turn will keep the drinks cool.

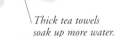
Try this with milk, water, and fruit juice.

1 Fill the bowl with cold water. Soak the tea towel in the water and wring it out. Wrap the tea towel around the bottles that you want to keep cool.

Plastic bowls do not heat up as quickly as metal bowls.

Make sure the bottle tops are closed tightly.

Thick tea towels soak up more water.

Deep bowls will cover more of the bottles.

2 Tuck the tea towel in between the bottles. This will keep them cool for longer, and will also stop the tea towel from slipping down.

Cover as much of the bottles as you can.

Make sure the bottom of the bowl is large enough to take all the bottles.

3 Carefully lift the wrapped bottles into the bowl. Keep the bowl in a shady place. When the water in the bowl warms up, replace it with fresh cold water. If the tea towel has dried out, do not forget to soak it again.

Storing rubbish

Burn all rubbish that you can, such as paper. Everything else must be stored and carried away with you. You should always leave your camp as if no one had ever been there.

Wrap rubbish securely so that you can carry it home in your backpack.

Remember to collect all the rubbish around your fire.

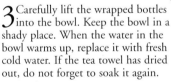

Crush boxes so that they take up less room.

Heat tin cans over your fire to burn off any food that might go bad or attract animals.

⭐ Wrap paper and card around sharp edges, like the tops of tin cans.

Carefully crush burned tin cans, so they take up less room.

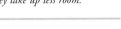

Sleeping outdoors

It can get very cold at night, so it is important to keep warm by maintaining your body heat. Most of your body heat is lost to the ground and from your head. Putting layers between you and the ground and covering your head will help to keep you warm or insulate you.

In hot weather, sleep in a sheet bag rather than a sleeping bag.

Materials

T-shirt   String
Bin-liners

Newspaper

Soft jumper
Thread ▮▮ Safety pin
Needle

Sheet

Blanket

Hints and tips

Most of your body heat is lost from your head and shoulders, so wear a hat on cold nights and pull your sleeping bag up over your head.

⛺ Ensure you always keep your sleeping equipment dry; if it gets wet, it will not keep you warm.

Making a sleeping mat

You need to make a thick mat so that when you lie on it, you are far enough off the ground to be insulated.

1 Fill a bin-liner with crumpled newspaper. Squeeze the air out of the bin-liner and tie some string around the top. Secure the string with a reef knot.

See page 54 for tying a reef knot

2 To make your mat waterproof, slide the filled bin-liner inside another bin-liner. Tie a piece of string around the top of this bin-liner and secure the string with a reef knot.

Use thick bin-liners that will not split easily.

Slide the knotted end into the second bin-liner first.

You may need to fill two to three bin-liners, depending on your height.

Make sure the blanket is big enough to cover all the bin-liners.

3 Lay the bin-liners end to end. Put a blanket over the top for extra comfort. When you sleep on your mat, the newspaper will absorb the cold and will keep you warm.

How to make a camp pillow with the T-shirt and the soft jumper

Lay the soft jumper out flat. Fold the sleeves in at the back and fold the jumper in half.

Slide the folded jumper inside the T-shirt to make your camp pillow feel comfortable.

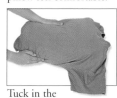

Tuck in the loose edges of the T-shirt and smooth away any bumps.

Making a sheet bag

A sheet bag helps you stay warm at night, and also helps to keep your sleeping bag clean.

Use an old sheet so that you can cut the end if it is too long.

1 Fold a single sheet in half lengthways. Make sure the sheet is long enough to cover your body and pull over your head.

☝ Be careful not to prick yourself with the needle.

2 Sew up the side and bottom of the sheet with two rows of running stitches. The inside row needs small, neat stitches as this is where the sheet will pull the most.

Use strong thread to sew your sheet bag.

☝ Running stitch is sewn in a straight line. The stitches and spaces between them are all the same length.

☋ See page 55 for tying a half-hitch knot.

3 Follow the instructions, right for adding the draw-string. Tie half-hitch knots in the ends of the string so that it does not slide back through the folded sheet.

When it is cold pull the sheet bag over your head.

Pull the draw-string and tie it inside your sheet bag.

How to make a draw-string for your sheet bag

Make a fold in the top edge of the sheet about 3 cm (1 in) deep to give room for the draw-string.

Sew two rows of stitches. Use small running stitches on the inside row. The outside ones can be larger.

Attach a safety pin to a piece of string and use it to guide the string through the folded sheet.

☝ Do not forget to remove the safety pin before using your sheet bag.

Buying sleeping equipment

Sleeping equipment varies depending on what you want to use it for. For example, sleeping bags can be made out of natural or artificial fibres. A natural-fibre sleeping bag will keep you very warm, whereas an artificial-fibre sleeping bag will dry out easily if it gets wet.

A track suit will keep you warm at night.

Buy a sleeping bag with a draw-string hood to insulate your head.

Choose a large, foam sleeping mat, as an inflatable one will puncture easily.

The zip should be well insulated, so it does not feel cold at night.

A curved back helps to keep body heat around your head, neck, and shoulders.

It is important to find dry wood for making your fire.

Making a fire

Fires are very useful. They will keep you warm and enable you to cook food outdoors. However, unless watched at all times, they can spread easily and become dangerous. Always collect all the materials you need to make a fire first so that you do not have to leave the fire once it is lit to collect more wood.

Materials

Dry grass

Matches

Dry leaves

Small sticks

Medium-sized sticks

Thick sticks

Hints and tips

When it is wet, look for dry, dead wood in the cracks of trees and underneath bushes and piles of leaves.

Use storm matches to light your fire in windy weather, because they do not blow out easily.

A wigwam fire

This kind of fire is very easy to make and can be used in most conditions. Choose a spot well away from anything that might catch fire.

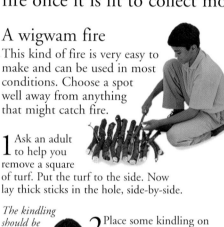

1 Ask an adult to help you remove a square of turf. Put the turf to the side. Now lay thick sticks in the hole, side-by-side.

The kindling should be bone dry.

2 Place some kindling on top of the thick sticks. Use small sticks the thickness of pencils, and small leaves. Build a wigwam shape around the kindling with thinner sticks.

Leave a gap in the front to add the tinder.

3 Put some tinder inside the kindling. Use dry grass, dead leaves, fungus, or bark as your tinder. Now light the tinder with a match.

⭐ If you have not lit a fire before, ask an adult to help you.

Use a ball of tinder the size of a grapefruit.

More details on how to make a fire outdoors

Find dry sticks that are about 5 cm (2½ in) around. Place them close together, side-by-side.

Use a good amount of kindling. It should not be squashed together, as it will not burn very well.

Balance the dry sticks against each other, with thicker, longer sticks on the outside.

Carefully light the tinder with a match. This will in turn light the kindling and the sticks.

🌽 Always watch your fire, making sure it does not burn too fiercely.

4 Once your fire is lit, it will burn very fiercely. The wigwam will collapse into a pile of very hot, flaming embers. When this happens, very carefully add more sticks. Thin sticks are best for cooking, and thick sticks are best for slow-burning fires to sit around.

Have extra fuel handy.

How to put out a fire safely using water, sand, or earth

Once the fire has died down, pour water over it. You could use dirty washing up water.

You could also sprinkle sand or earth over your fire to stop it smoking and put it out.

5 When you have finished using your fire, always put it out (see the instructions, above right). Carefully stir the embers with your foot to make sure there is nothing still burning.

🌽 Keep water or sand nearby, in case you need to put out your fire quickly.

🌽 In some areas, it is forbidden to make fires, so always check before you make one.

When the fire is cold, scrape the embers with a stick until they have all crumbled into ash.

Make sure you do not leave any rubbish around the fire that could harm an animal.

🌽 Always replace the turf you cut out for your fire when leaving your camp.

Keep your feet away from a burning fire.

⭐ Be very careful when stirring the embers; they could be extremely hot.

What you need for a fire

The secret of a good fire is to start off with very small sticks, and to gradually add larger sticks as the fire gets going.

Tinder
This is the most important part of the fire, as you cannot start a fire by lighting thick sticks.

Add to the tinder.

Kindling
When these tiny sticks burn, they set fire to the small fuel.

Small fuel
When this is alight, you have a fully burning fire.

Sticks the width of a finger.

Main fuel
Once the fire is burning fully, add the main fuel to keep it going.

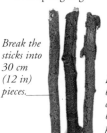

Break the sticks into 30 cm (12 in) pieces.

Large fuel
Logs are used for long burning fires and semi-permanent camps.

Logs must be burned completely before putting out a fire.

Cooking on a fire

Campfires get much hotter than kitchen stoves, so you must be very careful when you cook food on them. Always wait until the flames have died down a bit and the embers are glowing. If the fire cools down too much, you can always heat it up again by adding more sticks.

Smoke from the campfire will give your food a tasty smoked flavour.

Materials

Foil

Penknife

String

Twigs

Branches

Making a tripod

Always use a tripod placed over the fire when cooking with a billy can.

1 Wrap string around three sticks. Secure the string with a reef knot.

Try to find sticks that are about 1 m (3 ft) long.

See page 54 for how to tie a reef knot.

2 Spread out the sticks to form the tripod. Use a branch with strong twigs to make the pot hook. Strip off its leaves with a penknife.

See page 52 for how to use a penknife safely.

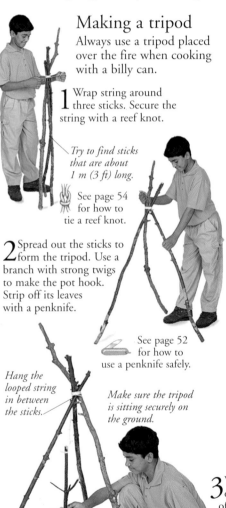

Hang the looped string in between the sticks.

Make sure the tripod is sitting securely on the ground.

Hang the billy can handle on one of the pot hook branches.

Details on how to make a tripod and pot hook for cooking food

Make sure you do not wrap the string so tightly that you cannot spread out the tripod legs.

Ensure the string used for attaching the pot hook is strong enough to support a billy can full of water.

Hang the billy can on different branches depending on how close to the fire you want it.

3 Wrap one end of a piece of string around the top of the pot hook and tie a reef knot in the string. Make a loop in the other end of the string and secure it with a reef knot. Now hang your pot hook on the tripod.

Hints and tips

Whenever you cook food in a billy can, lift the tripod and billy can on and off the fire together.

Use sticks the width of a finger to cook with so that you can control the cooking temperature.

How to make useful cooking utensils with sticks and foil

Make a toasting fork by stripping the bark of a Y-shaped branch and shaving the ends into a point.

Strip a long thin branch and shave the end into a point to make a skewer for cooking kebabs on.

Make a frying pan by wrapping foil around a Y-shaped branch. Squash the foil together.

See page 52 for how to use a penknife safely.

Different ways of cooking

One of the best things about cooking on a fire is experimenting with different cooking techniques. All you need is a few sticks, a penknife, and some foil.

Cooking sausages

Campfires get very hot and cook food on the outside quickly, but take longer to cook the inside. When cooking meat, it is especially important to make sure the food is cooked all the way through. If you do not, you may get an upset stomach.

Cut the meat into small pieces so that it cooks quicker.

Thread thin sticks through the sausages and put them on a Y-shaped branch.

Making meat kebabs

Cut tomatoes, mushrooms, courgettes, and fresh chicken into small pieces, and slide them on to the skewer. Cook the kebab for twenty minutes, until the meat is cooked.

Cook the kebabs on the grill made on page 32.

Cooking food over a fire with sticks and foil

Toast two slices of bread at the same time by putting them on to the sharpened Y-shaped stick.

Chop up vegetables and slide them on to the skewer, then cook them over your fire.

Cook fish in the frying pan. It is ready when the flesh goes white and the eyes cloud over.

Make sure you do not prick yourself on the sharp points.

Alternative cooking methods

Bacon in a paper bag
Poke a stick through the rolled top of a bag and hold the stick over a fire for 10 minutes. The bacon fat stops the bag burning.

Burgers in leaves
If you do not have any foil, cook your burger in a cabbage or lettuce leaf instead. This will keep ashes out of the burger.

Egg in moss
Carefully prick an egg with a pin. Wrap the egg in moss and place it in the embers of a fire for a few minutes.

All-in-one stew

When you are outdoors, you will probably be very busy during the day, so it is important to eat a hot meal and have a hot drink in the evening. Your body will be able to digest the food while you are sleeping, which will give you energy for the next day, and the hot drink will warm you up.

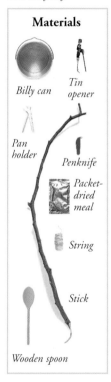

Always find the time to make a hot, filling meal every day.

Materials

Billy can

Tin opener

Pan holder

Penknife

Packet-dried meal

String

Stick

Wooden spoon

Hints and tips

Take dried herbs, curry powder, salt, and pepper with you; they will add a lot of flavour to your food.

Always eat everything that you cook; left-over food may attract animals to your camp.

All-in-one stew

This meal is very easy to make; just add your favourite ingredients to a shop-bought packet-dried meal.

The packet will tell you how much water to add.

See page 52 for how to use a penknife safely.

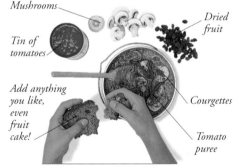

1 Soak the packet-dried meal in your billy can for one hour.

Mushrooms

Dried fruit

Tin of tomatoes

Add anything you like, even fruit cake!

Courgettes

Tomato puree

2 When the dried meal has absorbed the water, or re-hydrated, add all the ingredients (see the detailed instructions, right). Stir everything together and hang the billy can on a tripod over your fire.

See page 26 for how to make a tripod.

3 Let the stew simmer gently for one hour. When it is ready, take the stew off the fire and allow it to cool for a few minutes before serving; this will stop you burning your tongue!

More details on how to make the all-in-one stew

Using a penknife, carefully slice one onion and a clove of garlic into small pieces.

Open the tin of tomatoes with the tin opener. Make sure you do not touch the sharp, cut edge.

Crumble a stock cube into the stew to give it extra flavour, and to help thicken the stew.

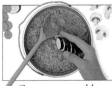

Cut your vegetables into small pieces, so they cook quickly, and add them to the stew.

How to adapt your tripod to heat water safely

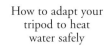

Wrap a piece of string around two of the tripod legs. Secure each end of the string with a reef knot.

Find a stick about 1 m (3 ft) long, and lodge it in between the sticks at the top of the tripod.

Wrap some string around one tripod leg and the stick. Secure the string with half-hitch knots at each end.

Hang the billy can on the stick by its handle. A stick with a strong twig at the end is ideal.

How to heat water safely

It is very easy to scald yourself on hot liquids, so always be extra careful when heating water over a fire. Adapt the tripod so that you can heat water much more safely over your camp fire.

See page 54 for how to tie a reef knot.

The twig on the stick is a useful hook for the billy can.

The string tied between the tripod legs makes the tripod more stable.

The string tied between the stick and tripod leg helps you to use the stick as a lever.

See page 55 for how to tie a half-hitch knot.

1 To adapt your tripod, follow the detailed instructions, left. Half-fill the billy can with water and hang it from the stick. Now lever the stick and billy can over the fire.

Hold the stick firmly when you are moving it so that you have full control.

2 When the water starts to produce steam, carefully lever the tripod away from the fire. Using a thick tea towel, carefully lift the billy can off the stick.

If you do not have a tea towel, use anything that will absorb heat and protect you.

⭐ If you feel unsure about levering the water on and off the fire, ask an adult to help you.

Hot drinks

When making hot drinks outdoors, the water does not need to be boiling hot; boiling water can scald you, and will be too hot to drink.

⭐ Always let any steam from the water die down before pouring it into a mug.

1 If you are making a packet drink with a dairy product in it, mix it into a paste with cold water first.

2 Hold the billy can of water with a tea towel. Carefully pour the water away from you into the mug.

3 Stir your drink to get rid of any lumps. Store it in a thermos flask if you want to drink it at bedtime.

More recipe ideas

When cooking outdoors, the main thing to remember is that some food takes longer to cook than others, so you have to allow for this when preparing a meal. For example, you would need to prepare baked potatoes and put them in the embers of your fire long before grilling a fish.

Experiment with lots of different camp recipes for exciting meals.

Materials

Wooden spoon

Fork

Penknife

Foil

Stick

Billy can

Bowl

Hints and tips

If you cook meat over the grill, watch out for the meat fat dripping into the fire; the fat will make the fire hotter.

Always take your billy can off the fire and wait for the steam to die down before testing your food.

Damper bread

This traditional Australian campfire meal is very quick and easy to make.

1 Mix some flour and water. Add the water a little at a time until it turns the flour into a dough.

Mix the dough in the billy can or bowl.

2 Keep your hands straight and roll the dough in between them to make a sausage shape. If the dough starts to feel sticky, add more flour to it.

See page 26 for how to make a tripod and pot hook.

3 Wrap the dough around the stick in a spiral and place it on a grill (see page 31). When the bread is cooked it will look golden brown and will slide off the stick easily.

Make a tight spiral shape.

How to prepare vegetables to cook over a campfire

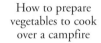

Wash the vegetables thoroughly in clean water to get rid of any soil.

Using your penknife or another knife, carefully slice the vegetables into small pieces.

Put the vegetables in a billy can of cold water. Hang the billy can on the pot hook.

Cook the vegetables in boiling water for about 15 minutes. Check if they are cooked with a sharp knife.

How to prepare a potato for baking in the embers

Wash the potato and then prick it all over with a fork to stop the skin splitting when it cooks.

Rub butter and salt on the potato. This will make the potato skin crisp and full of flavour.

Wrap the potato in foil and place it in the embers of the fire. Leave it to cook for one hour.

See page 52 for how to use a penknife safely.

Grilling fish

The best way to cook fresh fish when you are outdoors is on a grill placed over a camp fire.

See page 32 for how to make a grill.

1 Place the fish on the grill and then carefully lift the grill and tripod over a lighted fire.

See page 24 for how to make a fire.

★ If the tripod feels heavy, ask an adult to help you.

2 Watch the fish all the time it is cooking over the fire. If the fire is not hot enough, add a few more sticks.

Make sure the flames of the fire have died down a bit before you start cooking on it.

3 When the fish is cooked, the flesh will break into flakes easily. This usually takes about 10 minutes. Carefully lift the tripod off the fire. Use the spoon and fork to remove the fish from the grill as it will crumble easily.

Turn the fish over after it has been cooking for five minutes.

Food through the day

When you are outdoors, it is important to eat and drink regularly. Eat snacks throughout the day to give you energy and have your main meal in the evening.

Dried fruit and nuts

Boiled sweets provide lots of energy.

Biscuits

Baked potato

All-in-one stew

Hot drink

Orange

Apple

Water

Museli

Fruit juice

Chocolate

Breakfast
Always eat a filling breakfast and have plenty to drink. Porridge is ideal on cold days.

Lunch
Choose food that is easy to carry, like sandwiches and muesli bars. Pack sweet food for extra energy.

Evening meal
Cook something hot and filling. Use the heat from your fire to make a hot bed-time drink.

Making camp equipment

Pieces of camp equipment, such as stools and cooking grills, are very useful but bulky and heavy to carry around. If you know how to make them from natural materials, you will have less to take with you. Once you have made the equipment shown on these pages, experiment and make other useful items.

Simple camp equipment will make your camp more comfortable.

Materials

Sheet of plastic

String

Tent pegs

Waterproof tape

Penknife

Oblong piece of wood

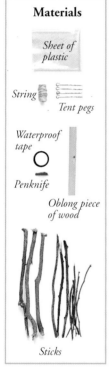

Sticks

Hints and tips

Flatten the tops of the sticks on the camp stool to make the stool more comfortable to sit on.

Keep your mud scraper close to your tent so that you remember to clean your boots before going inside your tent.

Making a grill

Adapt the tripod shown on page 26 to make a grill to cook food on over your campfire.

You could also use this grill to dry food, like fish, on.

1 Tie, or lash, three sticks to the tripod base using square lashing (see the detailed instructions, right).

See page 57 for tying square lashing.

Try to find sticks about 50 cm (1½ ft) long.

2 Use the three sticks lashed to the tripod as a base to lay smaller sticks across. The smaller sticks will form the grill.

Break the sticks to the correct length.

3 Lay the sticks side-by-side, close together. Use small green sticks, as they will not catch fire very easily.

Cook fish, damper bread, and kebabs on the grill.

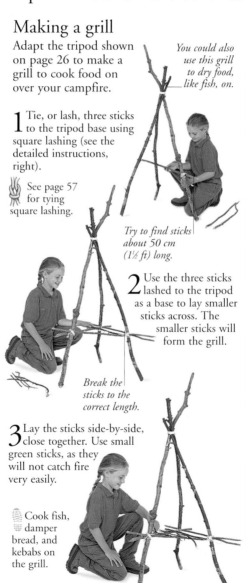

Details on how to adapt the tripod to make a grill

Take one of the sticks and lash one end to one of the tripod legs about 50 cm (1½ ft) from the bottom.

Lash the other end of the stick on another tripod leg. Repeat with the other two sticks.

Try to find straight sticks because bent ones will not support your food very well.

Make a criss-cross pattern with the sticks if you are cooking small pieces of food.

How to make the seat
of the camp stool with
the plastic and tape

Wrap string around the
top of each stick so that
it will support the seat
of the camp stool.

Fold the sheet of plastic
to make a triangular
shape and then fold it
over again.

Seal the open edges
of the plastic sheet
with some strong
waterproof tape.

Using a penknife, carefully
slice a hole through one
layer of the plastic sheet
in each corner.

Making a camp stool

You only need to pack the seat of
the stool; you can make the legs
when you are outside.

1 Take three strong sticks about 1m
(3 ft) long and lash them together
with string. Wrap the string around
the legs several times and then
secure the string with a reef
knot. Now spread the legs out.

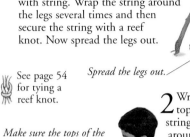

Spread the legs out.

See page 54
for tying a
reef knot.

*Make sure the tops of the
sticks are pushed out as far
as they will go.*

2 Wrap a piece of string around the
top of one of the legs. Secure the
string with a reef knot. Now wrap it
around the top of the second leg and
tie a half-hitch knot in the string.
Repeat on the third leg. Wrap the
string back around the first leg and
secure it with another reef knot.

See page 55 for
tying a half-
hitch knot.

*Push the top of the
leg into the cut
plastic sheet.*

See page 52
for how to
use a penknife safely.

3 Place the plastic seat of the camp
stool over the tripod legs. Make
sure that the three holes in the
seat slot over the three tripod
legs. This will keep the seat
secure when you sit on it.

Making a mud scraper

Keep your boots clean by making
a mud scraper for your camp.

1 Find an oblong piece of
wood. The top needs to be
quite thin so that you can
scrape your boots along it.

2 Push four tent pegs, two on
each side, into the ground to
hold the wood upright. You can
use sticks instead of tent pegs.

3 Scrape the bottom of
your boot along the top
of the mud scraper to
remove any mud.

Water in your camp

Collecting water is a vital job outdoors; you will need it for drinking, cooking, and washing up. Apart from rainwater collected directly from the sky, you cannot guarantee the water you collect will be clean, or sterile, so it is vital to learn the techniques shown here to be sure you always have clean water.

One way of ensuring the water you collect is safe to drink is to boil it.

Materials

Water bottle

Clean sock

String

Ground sheet

Sticks

Stone

Hints and tips

Leave water that you want to sterilize to stand overnight so that any sediment can settle.

It is important to have a constant supply of fresh water. If it is very hot, or you are going on a long trip, pack several water bottles.

Sterilizing water

Follow the instructions below if you do not have sterilizing tablets with you.

See page 26 for how to make a pot hook and tripod.

1 Hang the sock on the pot hook and place the bowl underneath it. Now filter the water by pouring it through the sock and into the bowl.

2 When the water has filtered through the sock and into the bowl, pour the water into the billy can.

3 Hang the billy can on the pot hook. Carefully lift the tripod on to a lit fire. Bring the water to the boil and boil for at least two minutes. When the fire has died down and the water has cooled, lift the tripod off the fire. You can now pour the sterilized water into a water container.

Cleaning water using a shop-bought sterilizing tablet

Put the sterilizing tablet in the water bottle. You will need one tablet for each half litre (1 pint) of water.

Let the water stand for one hour. The sterilizing tablet will dissolve and clean the water.

⭐ If the tripod feels heavy, ask an adult to help you.

Making a water collector

Rainwater is the cleanest natural water. Collect it as soon as it has fallen, using this water collector.

The sticks will lift the ground sheet off the ground.

1 Lay the ground sheet out flat. Make a small hole in the middle of one side. Tie a piece of string to this hole and tie the other end around a heavy stone (see the detailed instructions, right).

Attach heavy stones with string to each corner of the ground sheet.

More details on how to make your water collector

Thread the string through each hole and secure the string with a half-hitch knot.

Wrap the string around the stone once. Tie a reef knot in the string to secure it to the stone.

Make the hole on the front edge.

Use longer sticks at the back.

Use shorter sticks at the front.

2 Use the sticks to lift the corner of the ground sheet off the ground. Move the stones outwards so that they pull the sticks upright.

See far right for how to shorten the string.

This hole should not have a stick pushed through it.

Push each stick through each hole in the ground sheet, taking care not to make the holes larger.

The longer sticks make the water run down the ground sheet.

Shorten the string by wrapping it around the stone until it is the correct length.

Collect the rainwater as soon as it has fallen.

3 Continue adjusting the stones until the sticks are standing upright. Place the bowl under the ground sheet at the front to collect the rainwater.

The weight of the stone will make the ground sheet dip in the middle.

See page 54 for tying a reef knot, and page 55 for tying a half-hitch knot.

Storing water

Once you have collected your water and sterilized it, you will need to store it. Keep most of your water in a large container in the shade. When you are out walking, use a water bottle to store your water. Do not store anything else in these containers, and clean them regularly.

Collapsible water containers are easy to pack in your backpack.

Choose a water bottle with a clip so that you can fasten it on to your belt.

Using a compass

One of your most important pieces of equipment is your compass. It will help you to find your way, or navigate, so that you can hike through different kinds of land and get to your destination. If you do not have your own compass, you can make one by following the instructions on page 37.

A compass will help you to find your way when you are outdoors.

Materials

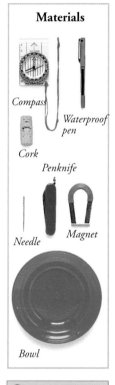

Compass

Waterproof pen

Cork

Penknife

Needle

Magnet

Bowl

Hints and tips

A circle has 360 degrees (°). North is at 0°, east is at 90°, south is at 180°, and west is at 270°.

Use the cord on your compass to hang it around your neck, so it is always handy whenever you need to use it.

Getting your bearings

Bearings are used to tell direction. You can use your compass to find the exact direction of an object by taking its bearing.

1 Put the compass on a firm, flat surface. When taking bearings, always keep the compass in the same place and swivel it around.

2 Place the objects around the compass. Look at the labelled compass on page 37 to see what the different parts are called.

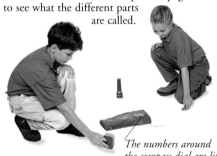

The numbers around the compass dial are like the degrees in a circle.

Practise taking bearings with different objects.

3 Point the direction arrow at the first object. Turn the compass dial around so that the blue arrow sits on top of the red north arrow. To read the bearing, follow the instructions, right.

This bearing is 250°, which is approximately west.

More details on how to find bearings with a compass

The compass has a magnet in it, so make sure you do not put it near anything made of metal.

Swivel the compass so that the direction arrow is pointing towards the first object.

The blue arrow shows you where north is in relation to the object that you are looking at.

The base of the direction arrow lines up with a number on the compass dial. This is the bearing.

Making your own compass

There are various ways to tell direction. The easiest is by using the Earth's own magnetic field. A magnetized needle works like a compass, swinging around to always point to magnetic north.

How to magnetize a needle so that it points north

With the hole, or eye, of the needle pointing downwards, stroke the magnet along the needle.

Make sure you always stroke the magnet down the needle. This will magnetize the needle.

Using a penknife, carefully slice a piece of cork. Now follow the instructions, right.

See page 52 for how to use a penknife safely.

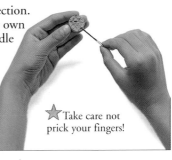

1 Carefully push the point of the magnetized needle through the sliced cork. If the cork is too hard, ask an adult to help you.

☆ Take care not prick your fingers!

👣 Use a waterproof pen so that the ink will not run in the water.

Point of the needle
Arrow showing north
East
West
Eye of the needle
South

2 Draw an arrow on the cork towards the point of the needle. This is your north point. Draw dots around the cork to show east, south, and west.

3 Half-fill a bowl with water and place it on a flat surface. Float the cork on the water. When the water has settled, the point of the needle will swing around to point north.

👣 Use a compass to double-check that the point of the needle is pointing north.

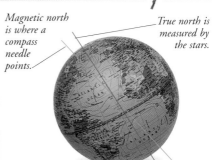

Protractor compass

You can find directions and take bearings with this kind of compass.

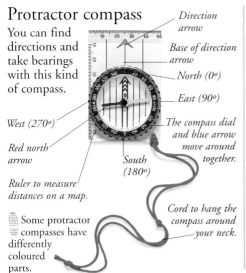

Direction arrow
Base of direction arrow
North (0°)
East (90°)
The compass dial and blue arrow move around together.
South (180°)
West (270°)
Red north arrow
Ruler to measure distances on a map.
Cord to hang the compass around your neck.

👣 Some protractor compasses have differently coloured parts.

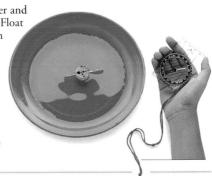

Magnetic north is where a compass needle points.
True north is measured by the stars.

Where is north?

There are three different kinds of north. True north is found using the stars, and magnetic north is where a compass needle points. Grid north is only marked on maps and map grid lines. It is in between true north and magnetic north.

Learn how to read a map so that you can navigate anywhere.

Reading a map

A map shows the position of an object and what the land, or terrain, is like. To use a map, look around you for landmarks, such as roads, rivers, or forests. Turn the map around until the landmarks on the map line up with the landmarks you can see. This will help you to work out exactly where you are.

Materials

Ruler   *Pen*

Compass

Card

Hints and tips

Grid lines are always spaced at equal distances on a map. If you know how much the distance between each grid line represents, you can work out distances on maps very quickly.

🏔 The upright, or 👣 vertical, grid lines on a map always point north.

🏔 Steep hills are 👣 shown on maps by lots of contour lines close together. On gentler slopes, the contour lines are farther apart.

The parts of a map

All maps are covered in symbols that represent the landmarks in the area. Look for a panel called a legend (see below) that explains what all the symbols mean.

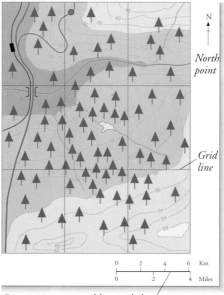

North point

Grid line

0 2 4 6 Km
0 2 4 Miles

Distance is represented by a scale bar. Here 2 cm = 2 km (1 in = 1.2 miles).

Legend

The symbols below make up the legend for the map above. Study the symbols so that you can understand the map.

● *Town spot*

—— *Road*

■ *Train station*

—— *Railway line*

Woodland

—40— *Contour line*

River

Lake

Marshland

] [*Bridge*

Contour, three-dimensional, street, and underground maps

On contour maps, the coloured lines join points of equal height, showing how the land slopes.

This three-dimensional map covers a small area in great detail, making it ideal for walking trips.

Street maps are used in built-up areas where you may need to get to your destination by road.

This section of a New York underground map is not drawn to scale. It shows where the stations meet.

Details on how to make a map of your area

To make the grid, draw straight lines across and down the page at 4-cm (1½-in) intervals

Keep the compass on the cross, swivel the compass so that it is pointing towards the first object.

Put a dot by the direction arrow. Lay your ruler along the cross and this dot and measure 8 cm (3 in).

Keeping the compass over the cross, point the direction arrow towards the second object.

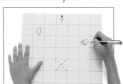

Continue adding objects until the map has got all the details you need to represent the area.

 Remember to add a scale bar and legend to your map.

How to make a map

Follow these instructions to make your own map so that you can record your surroundings.

 See page 37 for the parts of a compass.

1 Draw a grid and put a north arrow parallel to the upright, or vertical, grid lines, and a cross in the middle of the page. Put the compass over the cross and turn the map until the vertical grid lines align with the red north arrow on the compass.

Draw objects all around you; not just in front of you.

 For accurate steps, place the heel of your front foot butting up to the toes of your back foot.

2 With the direction arrow pointing towards the first object you want to record, ask a friend to take tiny steps towards it. Make sure she counts the number of steps.

 Use several tree symbols close together to represent a wood or forest.

3 Make your scale five tiny steps to 4 cm (1½ in). If your friend took 10 tiny steps to reach the object, you would need to measure 8 cm (3 in) along the ruler (follow the detailed instructions, left).

To make the scale more accurate, measure your friend's feet. If they are 20 cm (8 in) long, you can say that for every five 20 cm (8 in) steps taken, you will measure 4 cm (1½ in) on the map.

 Choose landmarks that are easy to recognize from a distance.

Make sure your friend walks in a straight line.

4 Now ask your friend to walk towards the second object and repeat what you did for the first object. Make sure she always starts walking from where you are sitting.

Finding your way

Protect your map by keeping it in a waterproof map case.

If you can use a map and compass together, you should be able to work out exactly where you are and how to get to your destination. A route card is also very useful. You can use it to work out how long it will take you to walk to your destination, and you can make notes on it about what to look for along your walk.

Materials

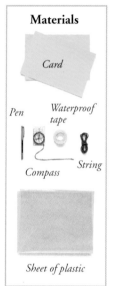

Card

Pen

Waterproof tape

Compass

String

Sheet of plastic

Making a route card

Mark your route on a piece of card following the instructions below.

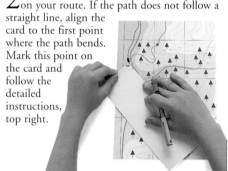

1 Place the corner of the card next to your starting point. Here, it is the train station. Draw a line down from this point, and a symbol to represent the station.

2 Pivot the card, so it aligns with the next point on your route. If the path does not follow a straight line, align the card to the first point where the path bends. Mark this point on the card and follow the detailed instructions, top right.

3 When you have marked all the points of your route on the card, align the edge of the card with the scale bar on your map. Divide the route into one-kilometre sections.

More details on how to make a route card for a walking trip

Pivot the card so that the previous point and the new point to be marked align with the card.

If your path crosses contour lines, indicating changes in land height, make a note of them.

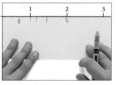

Using the scale bar, try to work out how long your route will take you to walk.

Use your route card to make sure that you have not chosen a route that is too long.

Make a note of any interesting places that you may want to look at on your route.

Hints and tips

Before setting off on a walking trip, always tell someone where you are going and when you expect to be back.

On level ground, you can expect to walk about five kilometres (three miles) an hour. Allow longer if you are walking uphill or on uneven ground.

Take a new bearing every 30 minutes.

How to make a map case with the sheet of plastic, string, and tape

Cut the plastic so that when it is folded in half it will cover a folded map comfortably.

Fold the bottom of the plastic up and seal it with the waterproof tape. Make two holes in the sheet.

Thread the string through the two holes and secure each end with a half-hitch knot.

Now slide the map into the plastic. Fold over the top and seal it with the waterproof tape.

The string enables you to hang the map case around your neck. Shorten it by tying a half-hitch knot.

See page 55 for how to tie a half-hitch knot.

Using a compass, map, and route card

When you are walking in new places, check you are going in the right direction by taking compass bearings regularly, using your map to help you find landmarks, and following your route card.

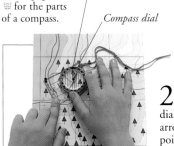

1 Put the compass over the point on the map that represents where you are standing.

See page 37 for the parts of a compass.

Blue direction arrow

Compass dial

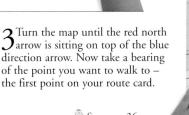

2 Keep the compass flat on the map and swivel the compass dial until the blue direction arrow is parallel to the grid lines pointing upwards, or vertically.

Red north arrow

3 Turn the map until the red north arrow is sitting on top of the blue direction arrow. Now take a bearing of the point you want to walk to – the first point on your route card.

See page 36 for how to take bearings.

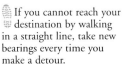

4 Turn to face the direction in which you are going to walk. Keep this point on the map ahead of you, and use the compass to maintain the correct bearing. Make sure that the red north arrow and the blue direction arrow are always pointing in the same direction.

If you cannot reach your destination by walking in a straight line, take new bearings every time you make a detour.

Using the Sun and stars

Even without a map or compass, you can still find your way, or navigate, by using your natural sense of direction, the stars, and the Sun. Find out if you live in the Northern or Southern Hemisphere, and then follow the techniques shown on these pages to navigate when you are out walking.

Use natural signs and your own sense of direction to navigate.

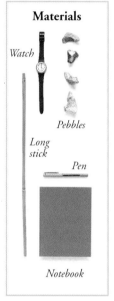

Materials

Watch

Pebbles

Long stick

Pen

Notebook

Hints and tips

The seven stars that form the tail and rump of the Great Bear are known as the Plough.

A constellation is a group of stars. The Southern Cross and Great Bear are both constellations.

The Southern Cross is in the misty band of stars called the Milky Way.

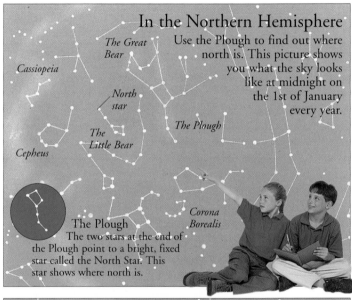

In the Northern Hemisphere

Use the Plough to find out where north is. This picture shows you what the sky looks like at midnight on the 1st of January every year.

The Great Bear

Cassiopeia

North star

The Little Bear

Cepheus

The Plough

Corona Borealis

The Plough
The two stars at the end of the Plough point to a bright, fixed star called the North Star. This star shows where north is.

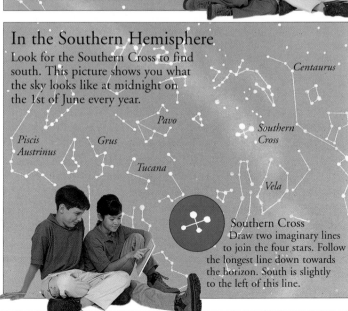

In the Southern Hemisphere

Look for the Southern Cross to find south. This picture shows you what the sky looks like at midnight on the 1st of June every year.

Centaurus

Pavo

Southern Cross

Piscis Austrinus

Grus

Tucana

Vela

Southern Cross
Draw two imaginary lines to join the four stars. Follow the longest line down towards the horizon. South is slightly to the left of this line.

Navigating with the Sun

The Sun always rises in the east and sets in the west, so you can use it to work out where you are. By making a sundial, you will be able to use the Sun to find directions.

Push the stick firmly into the ground.

1 In the early morning, push a stick into the ground. A shadow will form on the side opposite the Sun. Mark the end of the shadow with a stone. The shadow will be pointing west as the Sun has risen in the east.

How to work out where east, west, north, and south are

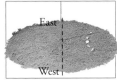

East

West

Using the east–west line you drew from the Sun's shadow, face east. North will be on your left.

North   South

South will be on your right. This is because south is always directly opposite north.

Use a straight stick so that it forms a straight shadow.

2 Use the stones to mark the position of the shadow at intervals through the day. In the afternoon, the Sun will move towards the west and its shadow will point towards the east.

The Sun's shadow creates a curve through the day as the Sun moves across the sky.

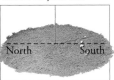 The closer you are to the Equator, the shorter your shadow will be. This is because the Sun passes directly overhead at the Equator.

3 Late in the afternoon, draw a straight line between the stones that you have been putting down. This line will point exactly east–west. Now draw a line at right angles to this line and straight through the base of the stick. This new line runs north–south.

Line that runs east–west.

Line that runs north–south.

Finding direction with your watch

By using your watch and the Sun, you can work out where north and south are very accurately.

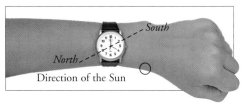

South

North

Direction of the Sun

Direction of the Sun

North

South

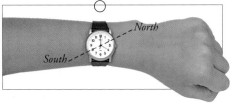

In the Northern Hemisphere
Point the hour hand at the Sun. South lies half-way between the hour hand and the 12 o'clock position.

In the Southern Hemisphere
Point the 12 o'clock position at the Sun. North lies half-way between this and the position of the hour hand.

Messages and trails

Sending messages and laying trails are important and useful outdoor skills. They enable you to let others know what you are doing and if you need anything. If you go walking without a map, you must leave a trail so that your friends know where you have gone, and you can find your way back.

Use natural materials to lay trails that only your friends can recognize.

Materials

Assorted leaves

Twigs and branches

Grasses

Stones and pebbles

Hints and tips

Use leaves, twigs, and branches that have already fallen to the ground.

Make the first signs easy to recognize, and later signs harder.

Write down flag signals as they are being sent and decode them afterwards.

Laying a trail

Use natural materials and change them in a way that only your friends will recognize, such as breaking a leaf or snapping a twig.

1 Before you start, make up a few standard signs, such as "turn left", "turn right", "go straight on", "take so many paces", and "no entry".

Do not forget to tell your friends what the signs mean before you set off!

Leave a "no entry" sign on a path you do not want your friends to follow.

Use signs together to make your instructions extra clear.

Use a sign to say "keep going".

2 If the path splits, make sure you leave very clear signs to indicate which path to take. Otherwise your friends may take the wrong path.

Use a "turn around" sign to make sure your friends do not go down the wrong path.

Signs you can make to lay on your trail

Make a square with four branches and put pebbles inside. Each pebble can represent one pace.

Make an arrow with three branches or sticks. Point the arrow in the direction you are going.

Adapt the arrow sign to make a "turn around" sign by adding two more sticks or branches.

A cross usually means no, so this is a good sign to use when you want to say "no entry".

Signs you can make (continued)

Lay a stick on a Y-shaped twig. Put a leaf on the end of the stick to point to the path you have taken.

Tie a knot in a clump of grass. Point the flowering top end in the direction in which you have gone.

Weave a twig into a leaf. This sign means "keep going". It is handy when the path is very long.

A leaf sandwiched in between two pebbles or stones could mean "hidden treasure"!

This is a very useful sign. It means "go home". You could use stones, pebbles, or leaves.

Practise laying trails and making up signs before you go off on an expedition.

3 Lay your trail on the side of the path so that the symbols are less likely to be disturbed. Make sure that your symbols stand out. If they do not, your friends could easily miss them.

Break a large stick into smaller pieces to make a "turn around" sign.

Turn leaves upside down to make the signs stand out more.

4 Make sure you lay a sign to show the trail has ended. If you do not, your friends will not know when to go home!

The knotted grass tells you to go straight on.

Sending flag signals

Flag signals are a great way to send messages to your friends when they are a long way off. Choose movements that are easy to understand, and always send the signals slowly; it is much harder to receive signals than to send them.

Always have a signal to say "send again" and "we understand".

Stand where you can be seen easily.

Simple movements could represent letters or whole words.

Tie your flag on to a stick.

Plant watch

All plants like slightly different conditions. If you know which conditions the plants around you like, you can tell all kinds of things, including whether it is usually wet or dry, and which insects and animals may be around.

Even the bark of a tree can provide clues about your surroundings.

Materials

Colouring crayons

Sketch book

Magnifying glass

Pencils

Pens *Torch*

Notebooks

Sunflower — Mullein

Sea holly — Rosebay willowherb

Bear's breeches

Yarrow

Iris

Hog-weed

Pretty flowers

Flowering plants need lots of water. If they are drooping and look wilted you can tell it probably has not rained for a while.

Wheat grasses

Cacti like very hot, dry conditions.

Unusual flowers

Even grasses and cacti have flowers. The wheat grasses above grow in most parts of the world.

No flowers

Mosses, ferns, and lichen do not flower. They all like damp conditions. Mosses grow on the shady sides of rocks, hill slopes, and tree trunks, lichen grows on the sunny sides.

How to press leaves so that you can record them

Choose a selection of leaves to press. Place them inside a book with absorbent paper.

Leave enough room around the leaves to label them and say where they came from.

Close the book and place a large stone on top of it. The weight of the stone will flatten the leaves.

Ferns cluster on damp ground.

Lichen only grows where the air is very clean.

Moss

Ecology box

Flowers die soon after they have been picked. To remember what they look like, draw them instead.

Plants grow towards the Sun. They grow towards the south in the Northern Hemisphere, and towards the north in the Southern Hemisphere.

Welcoming trees

A tree provides shelter and food for an amazing variety of animals. Owls sleep in holes in the trunk, birds nest in the branches, and hundreds of insects live among the leaves.

Different things you can find on trees

These rowan berries are brightly coloured to attract hungry birds and animals.

The clues that trees can provide

Deciduous trees drop their broad, flat leaves in the winter. They are common in warm places.

Coniferous trees have spiky, needle-like leaves. These trees often grow in cold, barren places.

The fruits and seeds of some trees are poisonous.

Squirrels make their winter nests, dreys, close to the tree trunk.

Spiders hide in cracks in the bark.

The trunk carries food down from the leaves to the roots.

Knot shows where a branch used to be.

Lichen shows there is very little pollution.

Lack of growth on the bark shows that this side faces away from the Sun.

The bark protects the tree's living tissues.

Lots of twigs grow on a tree's trunk, but very few will stay on the trunk and grow into branches.

Some fungi live in harmony with a tree, while others, like this honey fungus, destroy it.

When deciduous trees lose their leaves in the winter, you can identify them by their bark.

A tree's bark

If you do not know how old a tree is, studying its bark will give you some clues. The bark is the living part of the trunk and it changes as the tree gets older.

Making a bark rubbing

Young bark is very smooth.

Old bark often has ridges and cracks.

Young bark is under the flaky old bark.

1 Keep a record of the kinds of tree you see by taking rubbings of their bark. Make a note of each tree's name.

2 Place a piece of paper on the bark and gently rub a crayon over the top until you can see the pattern of the bark.

3 Note down the tree's name next to the rubbing. Take rubbings from other trees to build up a tree-record.

Animal watch

Take a torch with you so that you can spot signs of animal life.

Wild animals are frightened of people, and will usually hide from you. You can still tell they are about though, by studying all the signs they leave behind. Each kind, or species, of animal can be identified by its footprints. Droppings and dens can also give you a very good idea of which animals are around.

Materials

Magnifying glass

Pencils

Crayons

Torch

Pens

Tissues

Jar

Sketch books

Animal tracks

By studying tracks left in soft ground you can often tell which animals are in the area.

How to identify different types of animal track

Paw prints

Hunting animals have paws, often with claws. By looking at the shape and size of the pads, you can identify which animal the track belongs to.

This is a footprint of a domestic dog. You can tell this from the size and shape of the pad.

Hoof prints

Grazing animals, such as sheep, goats, and deer have hard, narrow feet called hooves. They can run away very quickly from dangerous animals.

This sheep's hoof has two toes with a space in the middle. It is called a cloven hoof.

Hopping prints

Small birds, such as crows and sparrows, are very light and have feet that are designed to grasp branches, so they hop instead of walk.

The open-toed print of this crow shows that it is a perching bird. The back claw grips on to branches.

Wading prints

Large birds, like ducks and geese, waddle from side to side as they walk. Their toes have skin in between them, making their feet webbed.

The joined edge of this duck's foot shows it has webbed feet, enabling it to walk on wet ground.

What animals leave behind

Detecting signs
of animal life
around you

Spiders' webs are
common everywhere.
They are easiest to see
in the morning dew.

Insects like woodlice feed
at night, so you will
usually find their tracks
in the morning.

Rabbits, like many other
plant-eaters, have
rounded droppings that
are very fibrous.

🔱 Birds leave rough-
edged holes around
nuts, whereas rodents
leave tiny teeth marks.

*Smooth body
feathers*

*Warm down
feather*

*Streamlined tail
and wing feathers*

Which feather?

There are many types of bird feather: fluffy
down feathers, smooth body feathers, and
streamlined wing and tail feathers.

*Tar spot fungus on this sycamore leaf
shows the leaf grew in polluted air.*

Tasty leaves

It is easy to tell when leaves
have been attacked by
caterpillars or fungi.
Caterpillars leave just
a skeleton of the leaf
behind and fungi
leave black spots.

*Cherry leaf
eaten by a
caterpillar.*

Gnawed food

Animals gnaw food in different ways, making
it possible to tell which animals are around.

*Hazelnut shells
eaten by
a vole.*

*Pine cones stripped
by a squirrel.*

*Winkle shells
gnawed by a rat.*

Animal
homes to
look out for

Wasps' nests are made of
chewed wood, and hang
from branches or holes in
trees.

Many birds build cup-
shaped nests in trees.
They weave all kinds of
things into their nests.

Some animals, like rabbits,
sleep in burrows that they
have dug underground.

Nocturnal animals

Unlike us, many animals are nocturnal. This
means that they sleep during the day and are
awake at night. Nocturnal animals include
foxes, raccoons, possums, gerbils, and moths.
Follow the instructions below to attract
moths at night, so you can study them.

🔱 If you shine a bright
light into the eyes of
a nocturnal animal, it
will be blinded and may
not be able to move
out of your way.

1 Loosely roll a light-coloured
tissue and slide it inside a
jar. A clear jar is best, so the
light can shine through it.

2 Place the jar on a firm, flat
surface. Shine a torch inside
the jar. Make sure it shines
through the tissue.

3 Moths will soon be attracted
to the lit tissue. Keep a
record of the number and sizes
of the moths that gather.

Weather watch

When you are outdoors, it is important to be able to predict the weather so that you are prepared for any changes. The wind brings changes in the weather, and you can predict these changes by studying the clouds. The size and shape of the clouds will tell you if it is going to be sunny or wet.

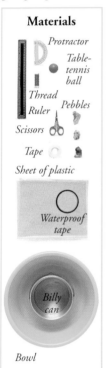

Learning to predict the weather can stop you getting caught in the rain!

Materials

Protractor

Table-tennis ball

Thread

Pebbles

Ruler

Scissors

Tape

Sheet of plastic

Waterproof tape

Billy can

Bowl

Hints and tips

A clear sky in the evening can lead to a very cold night because there are no clouds to keep the ground warm.

Insect-eating birds feed higher in good weather and lower when a storm is approaching.

Measuring wind speed

Changes in wind speed can indicate changes in the weather, so it is important to note what the wind is doing.

Tie about 50 cm (1½ ft) of thread in the middle of the bar.

1 Wrap some thread around the bar of the protractor. Secure the thread with a reef knot.

See page 55 for tying a reef knot.

2 Tape the other end of the thread on to a table-tennis ball.

Use strong tape.

3 Hold the protractor upside-down from the bar. When you hold the protractor parallel to the wind, you can read the angle the ball is blown to by the wind and so work out the wind speed.

30° = 50 kph (30 mph)

60° = 25 kph (15 mph)

75° = 10 kph (6 mph)

90° = 0 kph (0 mph)

How clouds can help you to predict the weather

A cirrus cloud is high and wispy. It is made of ice crystals, and usually means fair weather.

A cirrocumulus cloud is small, white, and lumpy. It is found high up, and usually brings fair weather.

A cirrostratus cloud is a thin, hazy, white or grey sheet. When it thickens, rain may be on the way.

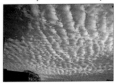

A stratocumulus cloud appears low down in the sky and can bring rain or light drizzle.

Using clouds to predict the weather (continued)

Altocumulus clouds are white or grey clumps, which may be separate or merged. They can mean fair weather.

A cumulus cloud appears in a blue sky in fine weather. It is white and puffy on top.

Cumulonimbus is a huge cumulus cloud, bringing showers of heavy rain and perhaps thunder.

Altostratus is a grey sheet-like cloud. If it starts getting thicker, rain may be on the way.

A hill-stratus cloud is a low, sheet-like cloud that covers hills. It produces fog at the tops of hills.

High clouds indicate good weather, whereas lower clouds generally bring rain.

Making a rain gauge

When it rains, a lot of water is absorbed by the ground. This makes it difficult to work out exactly how much rain has fallen. A rain gauge collects rain as it falls, which you can then measure.

1 Put the billy can in the bowl. Lay the cut plastic sheet over the top. The instructions, right show you how to cut the sheet.

2 Fold the plastic sheet so that the cut section is over the billy can and the rest of the sheet hangs over the top of the bowl. Secure the plastic sheet with the waterproof tape. Use the pebbles to weigh down the plastic sheet in the middle.

3 Tape the plastic sheet to the edge of the bowl. To work out the rainfall, measure the widest part, or diameter, of the billy can and bowl. The billy can used here is 16 cm (6¼ in) in diameter, and the bowl is 32 cm (12½ in). Follow the instructions, right.

How to cut the sheet and measure the rainwater collected

Fold the plastic sheet in four and then carefully cut a tiny piece out of the folded corner.

Push the middle section of the plastic sheet into the billy can. Fold and tape the sheet.

Divide the diameter of the bowl by the diameter of the billy can. In this case, it is 32 ÷ 16 = 2.

Measure the depth of water in the billy can. Here it is 1.5 cm. Now multiply this number by the divided diameters. Here it is 1.5 x 2 = 3, so 3 cm of rain fell on every 1 sq cm of ground.

Natural weather signs

Many plants are very sensitive to changes in the weather.

In wet weather, a pine cone will close up.

A pine cone will be open in dry weather.

In dry weather, seaweed shrivels up and feels dry.

Seaweed swells and feels damp in wet weather.

Using a penknife safely

A good penknife will help you to make all kinds of equipment, and is therefore an important part of your outdoor kit. However, it is vital that you learn how to use it safely so that you do not get hurt. You need to know how to open and close it and keep it sharp, as well as how to cut with it.

If you have not used a penknife before, ask an adult to show you how.

Materials

Leather belt

Sticks

Oil

Penknife

Sharpening stone

Hints and tips

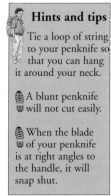

Tie a loop of string to your penknife so that you can hang it around your neck.

🔪 A blunt penknife will not cut easily.

🔪 When the blade of your penknife is at right angles to the handle, it will snap shut.

The parts of a penknife

A saw and tin opener are useful extras to have on a penknife.

Saw — *Groove*

A tin opener is useful. — *A good cutting blade is vital* — *Blunt edge*

Making a sharp wooden point

You may want to make different kinds of gadget for your camp. Once you know how to make a sharp point, you can adapt this technique to make all kinds of gadget.

Strips of wood

Hold the wood firmly.

1 Always cut away from you so that if the penknife slips, you will not cut yourself. Cut several thin strips of wood rather than one large chunk.

Push the blade in at a 30 degree angle to make a sharp point.

2 Use the ball of your thumb to gently push the blade away from you. Carry on cutting small strips of wood until you get a sharp point.

How to open and close a penknife safely

Put the nail of your thumb in the groove on the blunt edge of the blade.

Gently pull the blade as far as it will go. You should be able to feel it click into place.

To close the penknife, put the fingers of one hand flat against the blunt side of the blade.

Gently push the blade into the handle. Make sure the fingers of your other hand are not in the way.

How to sharpen the blade of a penknife safely

Rub some oil or water into the sharpening stone. Hold the sharp edge of the blade against the stone.

Stroke both sides of the sharp edge gently along the stone until the blade is very sharp.

Smooth the rough areas of this sharp edge by sweeping the blade up and down a leather belt.

Use the inside of the belt and ensure you always sweep the sharp edge of the knife away from you.

Stripping a branch

The branches you find lying on the ground will not always be exactly the shape you want. By stripping them, you can adapt them in any way you like.

1 Strip any leaves off the branch, and snap off any brittle twigs. Now decide which twigs you want to keep. If you are making a pot hook (see page 26) you will need to keep the twigs at the bottom of the branch.

2 Use the penknife to remove any other twigs you do not want. Hold the blade with the sharp edge away from you. Cut the twig at its base, pushing the penknife away from the branch.

3 When you remove the twigs, you will be left with small stubs. Trim these down with your penknife. You can also strip the bark by gently sliding the blade of your penknife along the bark at a slight angle.

A branch with no bark will dry out much faster than one with bark.

How to use the small saw on a penknife

If you need to cut through a thick piece of wood, use the saw on the penknife.

Hold the saw upright – if it is at an angle, you will not have as much control.

Pull and push the saw forwards and backwards until you have cut right through the branch.

Other cutting tools

If you are camping with an adult, you could ask him or her to make additional cutting tools for you.

Ask an adult to use these tools, as you could hurt yourself.

Making a wire saw
Bend a loop in each end of a piece of wire. Attach loops of string to the ends of the wire.

Using a wire saw
Use the looped pieces of string as handles, and pull the wire backwards and forwards.

Cutting with some flint
Sharpen the flint by dropping it on a rock. The flint will break and give a sharp cutting edge.

Useful knots I

There are hundreds of knots, each with different uses. However, certain knots have more than one use. It is better to learn just a few of these knots, rather than lots that you may forget or tie wrongly. You should also make sure the string or rope you tie your knot with is strong enough for its purpose.

Reef knots are used when ropes might get wet and be hard to undo.

Materials

Ropes of varying thickness

Hints and tips

Tying a half-hitch knot on to the end of another knot will make it stronger.

Tie a half-hitch knot into the end of a rope made from natural fibres to stop it fraying.

Artificial-fibre ropes will not rot as easily as natural-fibre ropes.

Natural-fibre ropes are easier to handle when it is wet and icy.

Tying a figure-of-eight knot

This knot can be tied very quickly and is very strong. It is good for tying loops.

This end comes over the top of the loop.

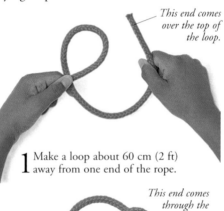

1 Make a loop about 60 cm (2 ft) away from one end of the rope.

This end comes through the loop.

2 Take the long, loose end over the top of the rope and the loop, then through the loop to make a figure-of-eight shape.

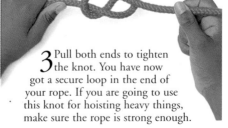

3 Pull both ends to tighten the knot. You have now got a secure loop in the end of your rope. If you are going to use this knot for hoisting heavy things, make sure the rope is strong enough.

How to tie a reef knot with two pieces of rope or string

Take two pieces of rope and bring the right piece of rope over and under the left piece.

Bring the red piece of rope on the left over the yellow piece on the right.

Tuck the red piece of rope under the yellow piece. Pull on both pieces of rope to secure the knot.

You can undo this knot easily by pushing the two ends of rope towards each other.

How to tie a half-hitch knot in a piece of rope or string

This knot is used to start many other knots and is handy for tying up loose ends. First, make a loop.

Bring the right-hand side of the rope through the back of the loop and to the front of it.

Now pull both ends of the rope tight. This will secure and finish the half-hitch knot.

See page 16 if you need to seal the end of a rope made of artificial fibres.

Tying a bowline knot

A bowline knot will not slip or tighten, making it good for tying safety loops when climbing or diving.

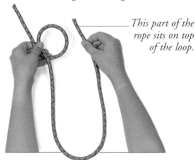

This part of the rope sits on top of the loop.

1 Decide how big the loop needs to be as you cannot change its size once you have tied the knot. Now make the loop.

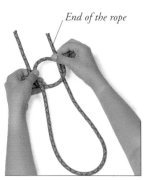

End of the rope

2 Bring the end of the rope through the loop you have just made.

3 Bring the end of the rope around the top of the rope and then back through the loop.

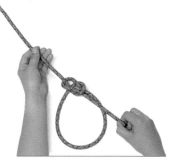

4 Now pull on the top of the rope to tighten the knot. This will secure the loop.

A sheet bend knot

Joining two ropes together requires a knot that will not slip, even if the ropes are different thicknesses. A sheet bend knot is the best one to use.

Make the loop in the thickest rope.

1 Make a loop with the yellow rope and slide the blue rope through it.

2 Bring the blue rope around the back of the looped yellow rope.

Keep the blue rope on top of the yellow rope.

3 Tuck the end of the blue rope underneath the part of it that crosses the looped yellow rope.

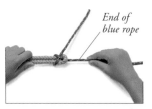

End of blue rope

4 Pull the end of the blue rope tight. The two ropes are now tied together securely.

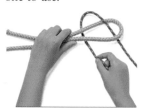

Useful knots II

The knots you use to tie sticks together are called lashings. There are many different kinds of lashing, each of which is suitable for a certain job. For example, shear lashing is ideal for joining two sticks to make a long pole, and square lashing is ideal for joining sticks at right angles to each other.

A timber hitch knot is the best knot for starting a lashing with.

Materials

String

Rope

Penknife

Hints and tips

When tying diagonal lashing, wrap the string around both sticks three times in each diagonal.

Leaving one end of the string loose (instead of tucking it in), will enable you to undo the lashing more easily.

Make a walking stick by attaching a small stick to one end of a longer stick with square lashing.

You can use shear lashing to make a secure tripod. Lash three sticks together and pull the string down in between each stick.

Tying a timber hitch knot

Both square and diagonal lashings start with a timber hitch knot. This knot is a variation of a standard half-hitch knot.

Short end of string

Long end of string

Loop

1 Use a piece of string to make a loop around a stick. Bring the long end of the string around the back of the short end.

Weave the long end of the string around the loop to make a twisted shape.

2 Twist the long end of the string in and out of the loop as many times as you can. You should be able to make three or four twists.

3 Now tighten the knot by gently pulling on the short end until the knot fits snugly around the stick. This knot can now form the basis of a lashing.

Short end of string

How to tie diagonal lashing on two sticks being pulled apart

Tie the string to one stick with a timber hitch knot. Wrap the string diagonally around both sticks.

Bring the string around the upright stick, then wrap it around the sticks in the opposite diagonal.

Now bring the string around the front and back of the sticks in a circular shape three times.

Wrap the string around the upright stick and secure it with a clove hitch knot (see page 57).

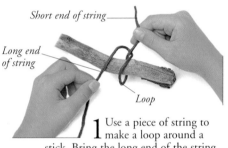

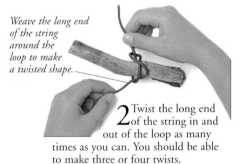

How to tie square lashing to two sticks crossing at right angles

Tie the string to one stick with a timber hitch knot. Now start wrapping the string around both sticks.

Bring the string above and below both sticks three to four times in a circular movement.

Loop the string around one stick, and wrap it around both sticks in the opposite direction.

When you have done this three to four times, secure the string with a clove hitch knot.

Tying shear lashing

Use this lashing to join two sticks that are parallel to each other.

1 Tie the string to one stick with a clove hitch knot, and follow the detailed instructions, right.

Strong string will make the lashing even more secure.

2 Wrap the string around both sticks. You need to cover about 3 cm (1 in) of the sticks. Now bring the string downwards in between both sticks and follow the instructions, right.

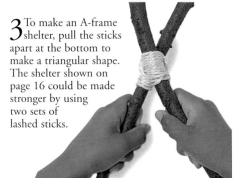

3 To make an A-frame shelter, pull the sticks apart at the bottom to make a triangular shape. The shelter shown on page 16 could be made stronger by using two sets of lashed sticks.

More details on how to tie shear lashing

Wrap the string around one stick several times, and then start wrapping it around both sticks.

Wrap the string tightly around both sticks. Make sure the string does not overlap.

Wrap the string in between both sticks three times. This will secure the lashing.

Secure the lashing by tying the string to one of the sticks with a clove hitch knot.

Tying a clove hitch knot

Use this knot to tie string to posts and other solid objects.

🦶 Use a clove hitch knot to finish off diagonal, square, and shear lashings.

1 Wrap the string around the stick once. Keep one end facing upwards.

2 Wrap the end facing upwards around the stick, and tuck the end through the loop.

3 Finish the clove hitch knot by pulling both ends of the string tight.

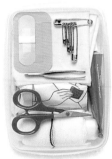

First aid I

You can help a sick or injured person to get better much faster if you know what to do immediately. This is called first aid. You need to be able to recognize when an injury is serious, so you can get help. If an injury is not serious, you need to know how to treat it so that it does not become infected.

A first aid kit can help to stop small injuries becoming infected.

Contents of a first aid kit

If you are going off hiking or are camping away from home, it is very important to take a first aid kit with you. The items shown here are all very useful things to have in your kit. Make sure you pack them in a clean, waterproof container.

Safety pins are useful for securing bandages.

How to treat cuts and grazes with a gauze pad

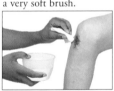

Gently wash the graze with soap and water. Use a gauze pad or a very soft brush.

Large roller bandages are useful for wrapping around injured arms and legs.

Gauze pads come in sealed paper wrappers, making them germ-free, or sterile.

Antiseptic wipes will disinfect injured skin.

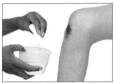

Try to remove any bits of dirt or gravel. Be very gentle, as this may cause a bit of fresh bleeding.

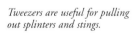

Triangular bandages can be used as slings.

Conforming bandages shape themselves to fit into the curves of your body.

Plasters help to keep cuts and grazes clean.

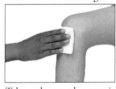

Take a clean pad, gauze is ideal, and apply pressure on to the cut or graze to stop it bleeding.

Tweezers are useful for pulling out splinters and stings.

Corn plasters will help to protect any blisters on your feet.

Calamine cream soothes sunburned skin.

Scissors are useful for cutting gauze and plasters.

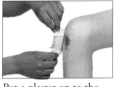

Put a plaster on to the cut or graze, making sure it has a pad large enough to cover the wound.

How to treat a wasp sting with tweezers and a cold compress

How to remove a splinter with tweezers

How to treat burns and scalds and protect them from dirt

You will need a pair of tweezers to pull out the sting. Hold the injured area to keep it still.

Wash around the splinter.

Make sure the water is not too hot.

Run cold water over the injured area until it stops stinging. This will take about 10 minutes.

Using the tweezers, grasp the sting as close to the skin as possible and pull it out.

1 Wash the affected area with soap and warm water. Be careful not to push the splinter in any farther.

Cover the burn with a clean plastic bag. If the skin is not broken, you could also use gauze.

Cool the area with a cold compress for about 10 minutes. Soaked gauze makes a good compress.

2 With a pair of clean tweezers, grasp the splinter as close to the skin as possible and draw it out at the angle that it went in.

Secure the bag loosely with a piece of tape. Ensure the bag or tape does not touch the burn.

⭐ If the patient is stung in the mouth, give him or her cold water to drink and get an adult.

3 Squeeze the wound to encourage a little fresh bleeding. This will flush out any dirt. Wash the area again, pat it dry, and put a plaster on it.

⭐ Remember never to put any lotions or creams on to the burn or scald.

Treating blisters

Foot blisters are very common when you are hiking. To prevent them, wear properly fitting socks and boots, and protect your feet with a plaster as soon as they start to feel sore.

1 Clean the blister thoroughly with soap and water. Now rinse it with clean warm water.

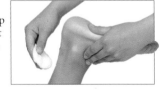

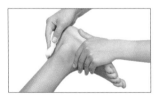

2 Dry the blister and the skin surrounding it by gently patting it with a clean pad.

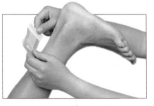

3 Protect the blister with a plaster that has a pad large enough to cover the affected area.

4 If the blister is very large, cover it with a clean, non-fluffy dressing.

First aid II

You can save someone's life if you know what to do and can act quickly. However, if you are unsure about anything, it is much safer to get adult help immediately. If someone is injured in a place that is dangerous for you to get to, you must get adult help straight away, even if you know what to do.

If the patient has hypothermia, wrap him up warmly.

Have a cold drink

Getting too hot or cold

When you are outdoors, your body is more sensitive to changes in temperature. You must be careful because getting too hot or too cold can be very dangerous.

Treating sunburn

Sunburn occurs when you have been in the sun too long without suntan lotion. If you get sunburned, move into the shade straight away, and apply a soothing cream, such as calamine cream.

Lie the affected person down in a cool place.

Sunburned skin is red and itchy, and feels tender.

Fanning will help to cool her down.

⭐ If your skin starts to blister or bleed, see a doctor straight away.

Treating heatstroke

Heatstroke can occur when the body gets very overheated. The affected person may get a headache, and feel dizzy and hot. Bring the patient into the shade and remove any outer clothing. Sponge her with cool water until her temperature returns to normal.

Leave the water to dry naturally.

Treating hypothermia

Hypothermia can occur if the body temperature falls. It can be very dangerous. The affected person will shiver and feel cold. The most important thing is to heat him up. Wrap him in warm clothes and blankets, making sure his head is covered. Give the patient a warm drink and some sugary food.

If you do not have a blanket, wrap him in a sleeping bag.

⭐ Do not apply direct heat, such as hot water bottles, on to the patient. He must warm up gradually.

How to recognize sunburn, heatstroke, and hypothermia

Sunburned skin looks red and sweaty. In extreme cases, it may even start bleeding and blistering.

Heatstroke makes the skin flushed and dry. The heart beats faster, making the pulse rate increase.

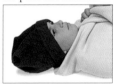

Hypothermia slows down the heart beat and pulse. The skin feels cold and looks pale and dry.

⭐ Ask someone to stay with him and get adult help straight away.

How to check someone's airway, breathing, and pulse

Check there is nothing in the mouth blocking the airway. Lift the jaw up and tilt the head back.

Check the breathing. Feel for breath on your cheek and watch to see if the chest rises up and down.

Gently press two fingers on the side of the windpipe to feel for a throb of pressure. This is the pulse.

⭐ If the patient's pulse and / or breathing does not seem normal, get adult help immediately.

Hints and tips

The windpipe runs down the centre of the neck.

🫁 If the patient's breathing is very shallow, place a mirror under his or her mouth. The mirror will cloud over as he or she breathes.

🫁 Make notes about the patient's condition so that you can tell an adult exactly what has happened.

Finding someone unconscious

An unconscious person will be lying down, not moving. Use the instructions far left to make sure she is breathing and has a pulse. Next, follow the instructions below to put her into the recovery position and then get adult help.

Shout to her to check she is not just sleeping.

1 Lie her on her back. Tilt the head back and lift the chin forwards to ensure her airway is kept clear. Kneel in front of her and bend the arm nearest to you to make a right angle.

⭐ If you think she may have hurt her neck, do not move her, just make sure her airway is clear.

Straighten the legs.

The palm must face upwards.

2 Bring the other arm across the chest. Hold the back of the hand against the cheek closest to you.

The hand supports the face.

Hold the hand against the cheek.

Bend the leg at the knee.

3 With your free hand, hold the thigh farthest away from you. Gently pull the knee up to bend the leg, making sure you leave the foot flat on the ground.

Keep this leg straight.

Make sure the lower leg is still straight.

4 Carry on holding the hand against the cheek. This will support the head. Pull the bent leg towards you so that she rolls on to her side.

⭐ As soon as the patient is in the recovery position, get adult help.

Use your knees to stop her rolling on to her front.

5 Gently place the side of the face on the ground, keeping the hand under the face. Pull the top leg out to form a right angle. This will stop her rolling over. Tilt the head back to make sure the airway is still open.

Countryside Code

When you are outdoors, it is important to follow the Countryside Code. This code tells you what you should and should not do to make sure that the countryside remains a place for everyone to enjoy. The most important points to remember are to respect wild animals and plants, and to take all of your rubbish home with you.

What you should do

Make sure you wear light-coloured clothes at night so that you can be seen easily. This is particularly important if you are walking on a roadside.

Reflectors and fluorescent bands will make you more visible at night.

Always close gates behind you. This is to make sure that animals cannot escape from their fields.

Always walk around fields if there is no footpath. If you walk across them, you may damage crops.

Fields often look free of crops in the spring, but there may be crops growing underground.

You should always be wary of animals. Make sure you find out about any that may be dangerous in your area.

This rattlesnake is one of the fastest killers in the animal world.

Rattlesnakes are the most dangerous snakes in America!

The headlights at the front of the car will light up the road ahead.

Be very careful with any fire you light; it could easily get out of control.

Even small fires, like this one, can spread very quickly.

If you are walking along a road, always make sure that you are facing the traffic on your side of the road. This is so that drivers can see you more easily, and you can see them.

Make sure you keep your dog on a lead so that it does not run around and frighten other animals.

What you should avoid

Take all of your rubbish home with you. Never throw it into rivers, ponds, or troughs where animals are likely to drink.

Never pick leaves or pull up plants; it is destructive and in some places, illegal.

This mother will be very protective of her young lambs.

Try not to make too much noise or play a radio or cassette player. Loud noises will disturb other people and animals.

Do not force your way through fences, walls or hedges; if you damage them, animals could escape.

You must not chase animals; they may hurt themselves or even chase after you.

Useful organizations

The Scout Association
Baden Powell House
65 Queens Gate
London SW7 5JS

The Guide Association
17–19 Buckingham Palace Road
London SW1 0PT

Youth Hostel Association
(England & Wales)
Trevelyan House
8 St Stephen's Hill
St Albans
Hertfordshire AL1 2DY

The Ramblers Association
1/5 Wandsworth Road
London SW8 2XX

Northern Ireland Scout Council
4th floor
38 Dublin Road
Belfast BT2 7HN

Irish Youth Hostel Association
61 Mountjoy Street
Dublin 7
61 Sraid Moinseo
Baile Atha Cliath 7

The Ulster Federation of Rambling Clubs
27 Slievegallion Drive
Belfast BT11 8JN

The Welsh Scout Council
The Old School
Wine Street
Llantwitmajor
South Glamorgan CF6 9RZ

The Ramblers Association (RA) Wales
Ty'r Cerddwyr
High Street
Gresford
Wrexham
Clwyd LL12 8PT

The Scout Association
Scottish Headquarters
Fourdell Firs
Hill End
Dunfermline
Fife KY11 5HQ

Scottish Youth Hostel Association Offices
National Office
7 Glebe Crescent
Stirling FK8 2JA

The Ramblers Association (RA) Scotland
Crusader House
Haig Business House
Markinch
Fife KY7 6AQ

Index

Acknowledgments

Dorling Kindersley would like to thank :

Erik Warren and Nick Dewdney for advice at photographic sessions; Gary Sanders for reviewing the synopsis; Carole Stott for checking the *Using the Sun and stars* pages; Brian Cosgrove for checking the *Weather watch* pages; Dr Rachel Carroll and Dr Simon Carroll for advice on first aid procedures; and Y.H.A. Adventure Shops for lending equipment.

Picture research: Jo Walton
Picture credits: T top; B bottom; C center; L left; R right;
Brian Cosgrove: 50 TR, CR, CRB & BR, 51TL, CLT, CL, CLB & BL,
John Cleare/Mountain Camera: 15TR & CR
Cartography: Roger Bullen, James Anderson
Illustrations: Nick Hewetson, John Woodcock